the world is not a rectangle

A PORTRAIT OF ARCHITECT ZAHA HADID

jeanette winter

Beach Lane Books

New York   London   Toronto   Sydney   New Delhi

In Iraq, rivers flow through green marshes.

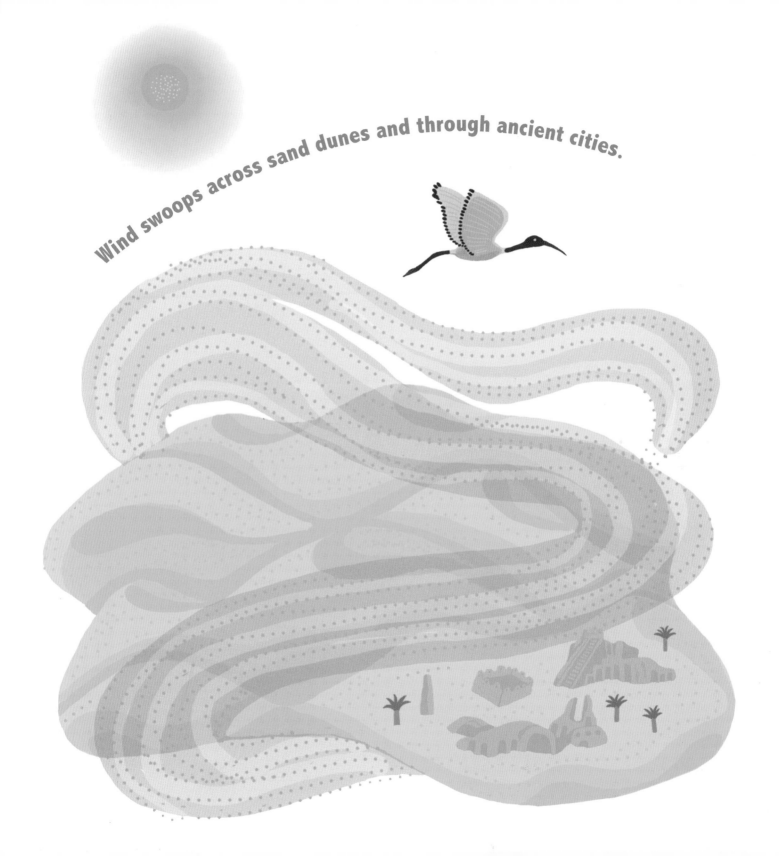

Wind swoops across sand dunes and through ancient cities.

Zaha Hadid sees the rivers and marshes and dunes and ruins with her father

and imagines what cities looked like thousands of years ago.

In Baghdad, where Zaha lives with her family,
she dreams of designing her own cities.

Zaha looks long and hard at patterns in her Persian carpet
and sees how the shapes and colors flow into each other,
like the dunes and rivers and marshes.

Zaha has ideas.

She designs clothes for herself.
She arranges her furniture.
She loves her mirror because the corners aren't square.

There are no corners in the dunes or rivers or marshes.

**Zaha is a Muslim
who attends a Catholic school
and loves math**

and still thinks about the ancient ruins.

She leaves home to learn more about cities and how to build them.

She has ideas.

In London, Zaha studies to be an architect.

She fills notebooks with plans and designs.

She makes paintings of the cities she sees in her mind.

**Zaha graduates with honors,
rents a room in an old school building,
and opens her own office—Studio 9.**

A few friends join her.
They all work hard—night and day—
making drawings and plans.

"We never slept."

Zaha's designs don't look like other designs.

Her buildings swoosh and zoom and flow and fly.

"The world is not a rectangle."

No one wants to build her unusual designs.
They say they can't be built, but Zaha knows they can.

So she enters competition after competition, hoping to win,
hoping someone will be brave enough to build them.

Finally, one of Zaha's designs is chosen.
The architect judges think her plan is best.

But the city committee doesn't like it
and won't build it.
They hold another competition, her design wins again,
and STILL they refuse.

Hadid means *iron* in Arabic,
and Zaha is strong as iron.
She keeps on working—one plan after another.
"I made a conscious decision not to stop."

Zaha remembers the grasses in the marshes swaying

and sees tall buildings dancing like grass.

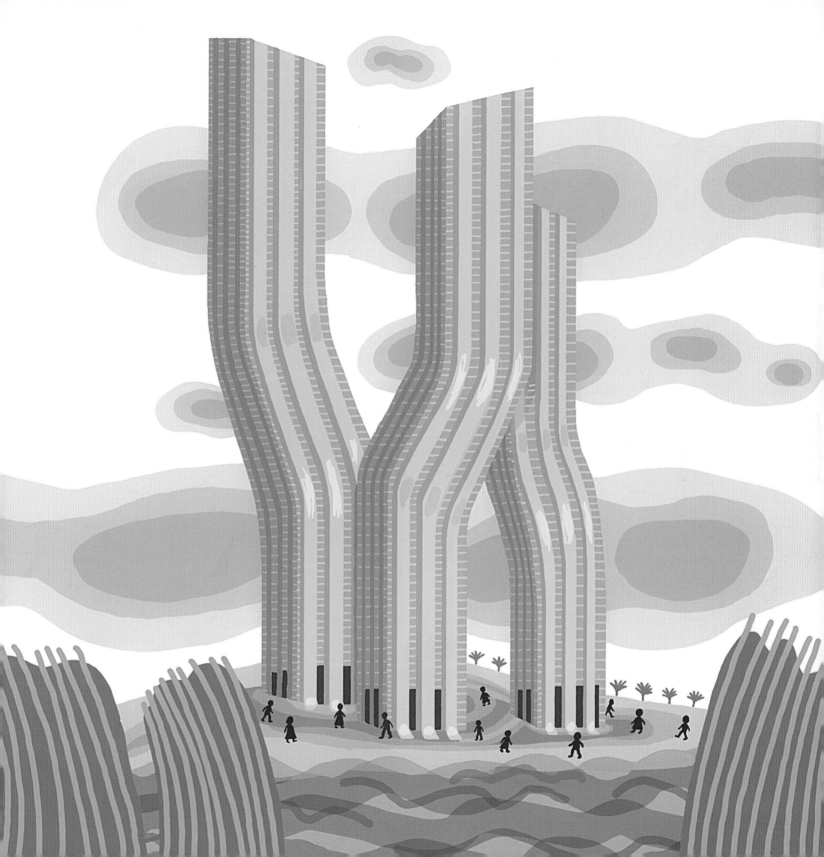

Zaha remembers the wind in the dune.

and feels it blowing over and around and through her desert building.

Zaha looks at shells and cradles her stadium like a cocoon.

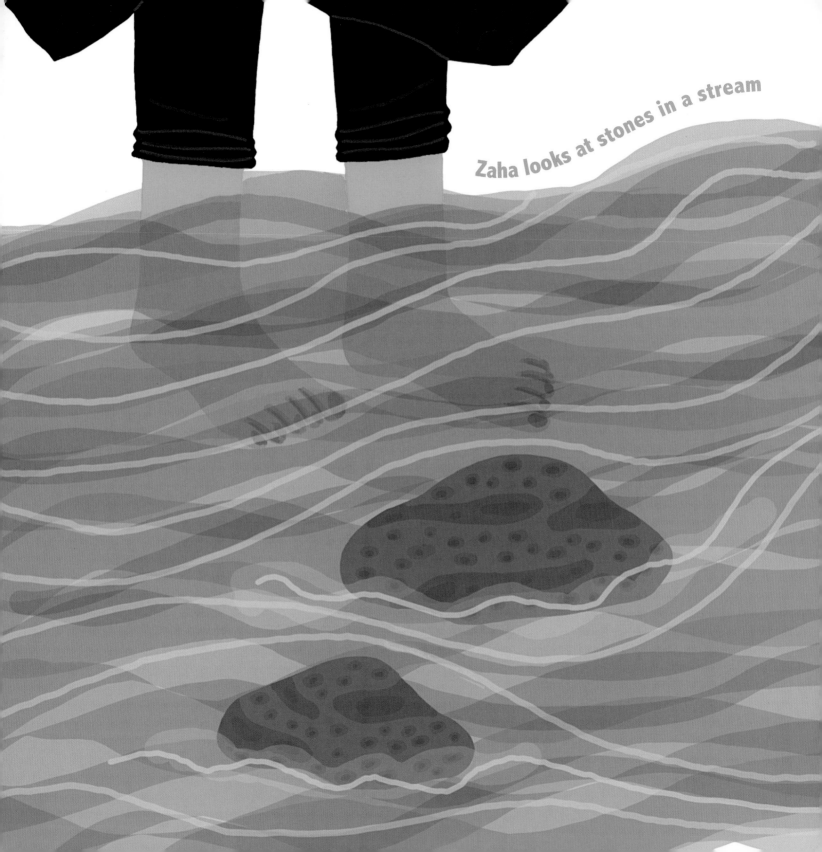

Zaha looks at stones in a stream

and builds an opera house like the pebbles in the water.

Inside the opera house, a singe

s the pearl in the oyster shell.

Zaha looks up at stars and galaxies
and sees swirling buildings.

Zaha looks at waves and sees a bridge that moves with the water.

Zaha looks at the Alps

and builds a museum inside a mountain peak

with windows to see the sky and the valleys.

Zaha's ski jump reaches to the sky like the mountains.

Zaha thinks of the jungle and ancient wood temples

and builds a wooden building to remember a faraway war.

One by one, Zaha's designs become buildings
all over the world.

"We do this so you can be in a simple place and feel good."

Zaha is so busy now that every room in the old school building is filled.

Over four hundred architects work in these rooms—
designing, planning, engineering, and making models
of Zaha's visions.

"You should do what you like."

Zaha designs a dollhouse,

and shoes,

and chairs.

She designs
a stalactite sculpture

and an iceberg seat.

"I can't stop thinking."

Sometimes when she is working,
Zaha's early memories return.

"The beauty of the landscape—
where sand, water, reeds, birds, buildings, and people
all somehow flow together—has never left me."

"I still believe in the impossible."

Then one night, the light in Zaha's window goes dark.
She has left this world.

But her architects keep their lights on—
designing, planning, engineering, and making models of her visions,
keeping her flame blazing bright.

Even though Zaha is gone.

What are they? Where are they?

Cardiff Bay Opera House
Cardiff, Wales
(never built)

Al Wakrah Stadium
Qatar

Signature Towers
Dubai, United Arab Emirates

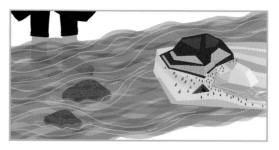

Guangzhou Opera House
Guangzhou, China

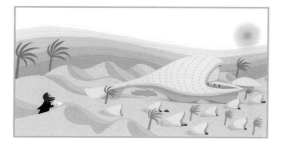

Bee'ah Headquarters
Sharjah, United Arab Emirates

Galaxy Soho
Beijing, China

Bergisel Ski Jump
Innsbruck, Austria

Sheikh Zayed Bridge
Abu Dhabi, United Arab Emirates

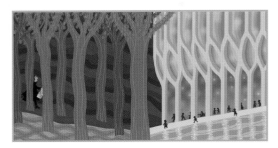

Sleuk Rith Institute
Phnom Penh, Cambodia

Messner Mountain Museum Corones
Province of Bolzano, South Tyrol, Italy

Zaha was daring.

"The world is not a rectangle. You don't go into a park and say: 'My God, we don't have any corners.'"

Zaha was original.

"My work is not within the accepted box. Maybe because I am a woman. Also an Arab."

Zaha spoke her mind.

"As a woman, I'm expected to want everything to be nice, and to be nice myself.... I don't design nice buildings—I don't like them."

Zaha Mohammad Hadid was born in Baghdad, Iraq, on October 31, 1950, and she died in Miami, Florida, on March 31, 2016. She was sixty-five years old.

Zaha had degrees in mathematics and architecture. She lived in London and was made a Dame Commander of the Order of the British Empire in 2012.

Among the many awards and honors Zaha received in her lifetime were the Pritzker Prize—the most prestigious architecture award in the world—and the Royal Institute of British Architects Royal Gold Medal, the top architecture award in Britain.

She was the first woman ever to receive these awards.

AUTHOR'S NOTE

When I first saw photos of Zaha Hadid's architectural designs in 2010, the buildings seemed to fly. My spirit also took flight—to a place in my imagination that only landscape had taken me before. I had to find out more about her.

—J. W.

SOURCES

Barber, Lynn. "Lynn Barber Meets Zaha Hadid." *The Guardian*. March 9, 2008. https://www.theguardian.com /lifeandstyle/2008/mar/09/women.architecture.

Brooks, Xan. "Zaha Hadid: 'I Don't Make Nice Little Buildings.'" *The Guardian*. September 22, 2013. https:// www.theguardian.com/artanddesign/2013/sep/22/zaha-hadid-dont-make-nice-little-buildings.

Elkann, Alain. "Zaha Hadid: It's Tough Being an Arab Woman in the Architecture Business." *The Huffington Post*. May 9, 2015. http://www.huffingtonpost.com/alain-elkann/zaha-hadid-arab-architecture_b_6811334.html.

Glancey, Jonathan. "Zaha Hadid on the Trials of Being a Woman Architect." *The Guardian*. October 9, 2006. https:// www.theguardian.com/artanddesign/2006/oct/09/architecture.communities.

Hadid, Zaha. "Dame Zaha Hadid in Conversation." Interviewed by Juliet Sprake. YouTube video, 9:06. Posted by "Goldsmiths University of London," October 14, 2014. https://www.youtube.com/watch?v=t82U23b71ck.

———. "Interview with Zaha Hadid." YouTube video, 13:02. Posted by "Baku Magazine," February 4, 2014. https:// www.youtube.com/watch?v=ZaHyKOhammk.

———. "Interview: Zaha Hadid at Dezeen Studio." Interviewed by Marcus Fairs. YouTube video, 5:28. Posted by "Dezeen," January 14, 2013. https://www.youtube.com/watch?v=13Og4EZpXiI.

———. "Maison & Objet 2008: Zaha Hadid (Interview)." YouTube video, 4:30. Posted by "MoebelKulturKanal," August 27, 2010. https://www.youtube.com/watch?v=WFLjoiEVac8.

———. "The Story of Wangjing SOHO: Exclusive Dialogue with Zhang Xin and Zaha Hadid." Interviewed by Zhang Xin. YouTube video, 6:30. Posted by "SOHO China," October 8, 2014. https://www.youtube.com /watch?v=LcPy6JCCAGk.

———. "Visions and Voices: An Evening with Zaha Hadid." YouTube video, 1:35:16. Posted by "USC," November 12, 2014. https://www.youtube.com/watch?v=mvEwSPkncB4.

———. "Waraa Al Woojooh—Zaha Hadid." Interviewed by Ricardo Karam. YouTube video, 58:52. Posted by "Ricardo Karam," January 27, 2014. https://www.youtube.com/watch?v=Av__gx3i8vc.

———. "What Is New?—Zaha Hadid." YouTube video, 1:14:25. Posted by "Columbia GSAPP," January 11, 2012. https:// www.youtube.com/watch?v=O7j7gTBqijA.

———. "Zaha Hadid." YouTube video, 1:24:42. Posted by "Harvard GSD," March 18, 2013. https://www.youtube.com /watch?v=DhHiYU3kLOE.

———. *Zaha Hadid: Complete Works*. New York: Rizzoli, 2009.

———. "Zaha Hadid Talking about Challenges of Architecture." YouTube video, 6:31. Posted by "JOMagazine2003," April 5, 2010. https://www.youtube.com/watch?v=QcdvMm6c-fU.

———. "Zaha Hadid. Who Dares Wins. Architecture Documentary." YouTube video, 1:09:37. Posted by "artandfilm21," January 5, 2016. https://www.youtube.com/watch?v=SOd5tiAKBs0.

Hadid, Zaha, and Aaron Betsky. *Zaha Hadid: The Complete Buildings and Projects*. New York: Rizzoli, 1998.

Moore, Rowan. "Zaha Hadid: Queen of the Curve." *The Guardian*. September 7, 2013. https://www.theguardian.com /artanddesign/2013/sep/08/zaha-hadid-serpentine-sackler-profile.

Seabrook, John. "The Abstractionist: Zaha Hadid's Unfettered Invention." *New Yorker*. December 21, 2009. http:// www.newyorker.com/magazine/2009/12/21/the-abstractionist.

Trickey, Erick. "Zaha Hadid Biography." In *Encyclopedia of World Biography*. Advameg, Inc. Accessed March 3, 2010. http://www.notablebiographies.com/newsmakers2/2005-Fo-La/Hadid-Zaha.html.

For AJ & AB—
and in memory of Zaha Hadid

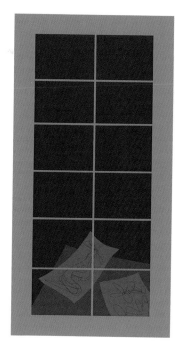

BEACH LANE BOOKS • An imprint of Simon & Schuster Children's Publishing Division • 1230 Avenue of the Americas, New York, New York 10020 • Copyright © 2017 by Jeanette Winter • All rights reserved, including the right of reproduction in whole or in part in any form. • **BEACH LANE BOOKS** is a trademark of Simon & Schuster, Inc. • For information about special discounts for bulk purchases, please contact Simon & Schuster Special Sales at 1-866-506-1949 or business@simonandschuster.com. • The Simon & Schuster Speakers Bureau can bring authors to your live event. For more information or to book an event, contact the Simon & Schuster Speakers Bureau at 1-866-248-3049 or visit our website at www.simonspeakers.com. • Book design by Ann Bobco • The text for this book was set in Abadi MT Condensed. • Manufactured in China • 0617 SCP • First Edition • 10 9 8 7 6 5 4 3 2 1 • Library of Congress Cataloging-in-Publication Data Names: Winter, Jeanette, author. • Title: The world is not a rectangle : a portrait of architect Zaha Hadid / Jeanette Winter. • Description: New York : Beach Lane Books, 2017. | Includes bibliographical references • Identifiers: LCCN 2016048805| ISBN 9781481446693 (hardcover : alk. paper) | ISBN 9781481446709 (e-book) • Subjects: LCSH: Hadid, Zaha. | Architects—Iraq—Biography—Juvenile literature. | Architecture, Modern—20th century—Juvenile literature. | Architecture, Modern—21st century—Juvenile literature. • Classification: LCC NA1469.H33 W56 2017 | DDC 720.92 [B] —dc23 LC record available at https://lccn.loc.gov/2016048805